KOLMANSKOP

THE DIAMOND MINE GHOST TOWN

BY CHRISTINA LEAF

Torque brims with excitement
perfect for thrill-seekers of all kinds.
Discover daring survival skills, explore
uncharted worlds, and marvel at mighty
engines and extreme sports. In *Torque* books,
anything can happen. Are you ready?

This edition first published in 2020 by Bellwether Media, Inc.

No part of this publication may be reproduced in whole or in part without written permission of the publisher. For information regarding permission, write to Bellwether Media, Inc., Attention: Permissions Department, 6012 Blue Circle Drive, Minnetonka, MN 55343.

Library of Congress Cataloging-in-Publication Data

Names: Leaf, Christina, author.
Title: Kolmanskop : the diamond mine ghost town / Christina Leaf.
Other titles: Abandoned places.
Description: Minneapolis, MN : Bellwether Media, 2020. | Series: Abandoned places | Includes bibliographical references and index. | Audience: Ages 7-12 | Audience: Grades 4-6 | Summary: ""Amazing photography accompanies engaging information about Kolmanskop. The combination of high-interest subject matter and light text is intended for students in grades 3 through 7"–Provided by publisher"– Provided by publisher.
Identifiers: LCCN 2019030604 (print) | LCCN 2019030605 (ebook) | ISBN 9781644871614 (library binding) | ISBN 9781618918314 (ebook)
Subjects: LCSH: Diamond mines and mining–Namibia–Namib Desert–Juvenile literature. | Ghost towns–Namibia–Namib Desert–Juvenile literature. | Kolmanskop (Namibia)–History–Juvenile literature.
Classification: LCC DT1685.K65 L43 2020 (print) | LCC DT1685.K65 (ebook) | DDC 916.881–dc23
LC record available at https://lccn.loc.gov/2019030604
LC ebook record available at https://lccn.loc.gov/2019030605

Text copyright © 2020 by Bellwether Media, Inc. TORQUE and associated logos are trademarks and/or registered trademarks of Bellwether Media, Inc.

Editor: Betsy Rathburn   Designer: Brittany McIntosh

Printed in the United States of America, North Mankato, MN.

TABLE OF CONTENTS

THE SANDS OF TIME

You step off the tour bus into the baking sun of the Namib Desert. A worn sign stands outside of a small settlement. Its old-fashioned letters welcome you to *Kolmannskuppe,* or Kolmanskop.

Coleman's Hill
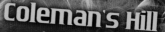

Kolmanskop comes from the German word for Coleman's Hill. Stories say a worker named Coleman left his oxcart on a nearby hill after it broke down.

Just beyond the sign, shabby houses stand in the sands of the desert. Their empty windows show only darkness.

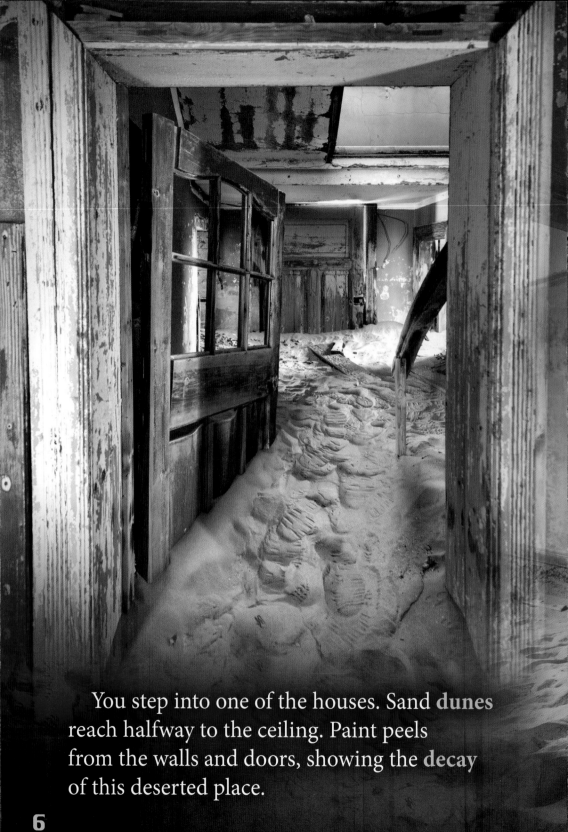

You step into one of the houses. Sand **dunes** reach halfway to the ceiling. Paint peels from the walls and doors, showing the **decay** of this deserted place.

You wonder what Kolmanskop looked like when it brimmed with wealth. How long will it take for the desert sands to swallow this town completely?

A DIAMOND IN THE ROUGH

Kolmanskop is a **ghost town** in the Namib Desert of Namibia. It lies just east of a coastal town called Lüderitz.

Kolmanskop,
Namibia

Kolmanskop was once a diamond mining **boomtown**. At the time, it was in the German **colony** of South West Africa. In less than 50 years, Kolmanskop would reach great heights and then fall into abandonment.

At its peak, Kolmanskop was home to around 1,300 people. The population was not very big. But Kolmanskop was one of the richest towns in the world!

Wild Ostrich Chase

One family owned an ostrich. It pulled a sleigh across the dunes on Christmas!

German colonists shaped the town. They fashioned buildings in the style of their home country. But most of Kolmanskop's people were Namibian **miners**.

A BRIGHT FUTURE

In 1908, a worker named Zacherias Lewala made an exciting discovery. He found a shiny stone while he was shoveling sand off the railroad tracks. His boss realized it was a diamond!

Share the Wealth

Lewala did not earn money from his discovery. In fact, most Namibian workers earned little from the diamonds they found.

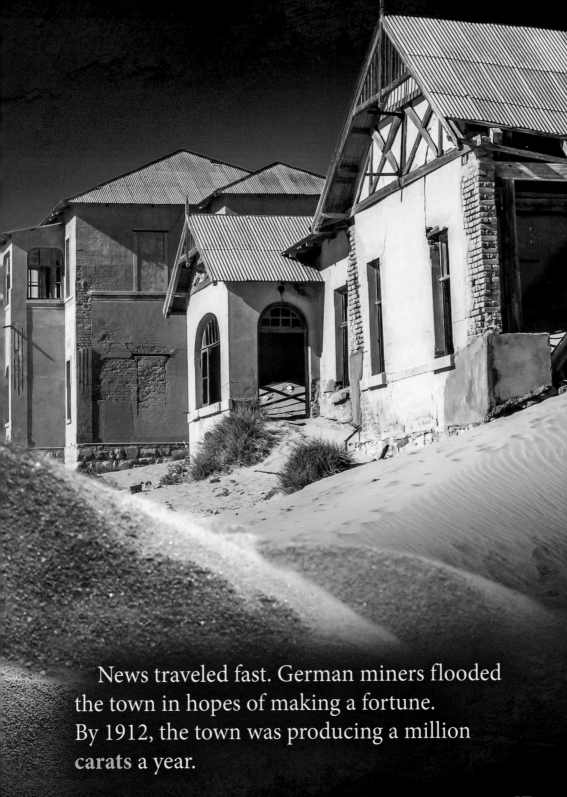

News traveled fast. German miners flooded the town in hopes of making a fortune. By 1912, the town was producing a million **carats** a year.

The German colonists lost little time in making Kolmanskop comfortable. They built large, fancy houses. Workers swept the sand from the streets each day. Water came in by train.

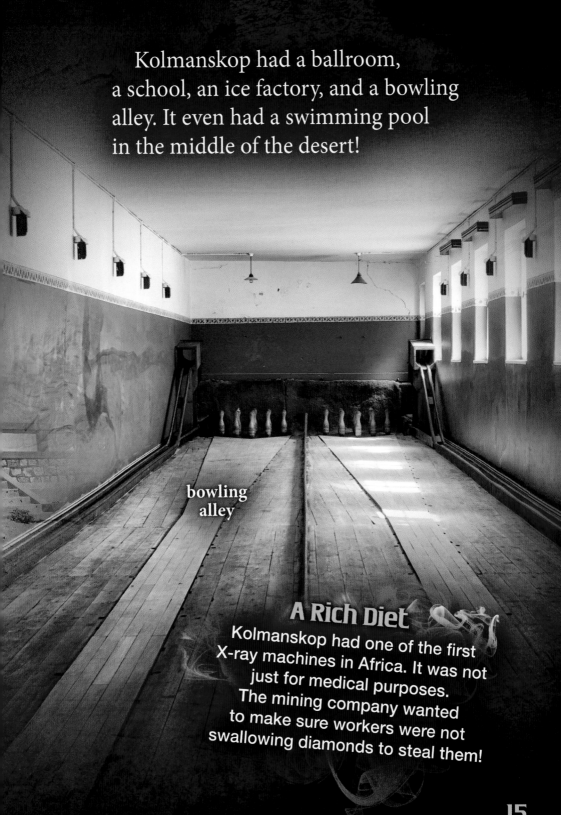

Kolmanskop had a ballroom, a school, an ice factory, and a bowling alley. It even had a swimming pool in the middle of the desert!

bowling alley

A Rich Diet

Kolmanskop had one of the first X-ray machines in Africa. It was not just for medical purposes. The mining company wanted to make sure workers were not swallowing diamonds to steal them!

KOLMANSKOP TIMELINE

1908:
Zacherias Lewala discovers a shiny stone that turns out to be a diamond

1930:
Diamond mining stops at Kolmanskop

1928:
Another diamond field is discovered south of Kolmanskop

At first, diamonds were everywhere! Workers could easily find them in the sand. A diamond mining company quickly **restricted** the area. Miners could not search without the company's permission.

By 1918, there were few diamonds left to be found. Later, a bigger diamond field was found far from the town.

Moon Stones
People could even hunt for diamonds at night. The stones shone in the moonlight!

2002:
Kolmanskop becomes a tourist attraction

1956:
The last families leave the town

DESERTED IN THE DESERT

At the news of the new diamond field, many families picked up and left. Some did not even bother to take all of their possessions. By 1930, diamond production in Kolmanskop had stopped entirely.

The last few families left the town in 1956. For **decades**, the abandoned town was left to bake under the hot Namib Desert sun.

**restored
dining room**

Today, the mining company still shares
ownership of the land. In the 1980s, it **restored**
some of the buildings. It also built a museum

Despite the restorations, many houses still sit in disrepair. Belongings from long-gone families can be found buried under the sand. Kolmanskop shows us how quickly nature can reclaim its land.

GLOSSARY

boomtown—a town that has a sudden population increase due to business growth

carats—units of measurement for precious stones

colony—a territory claimed and settled by people from a country far away

decades—tens of years

decay—breakdown or ruin

dunes—hills of sand

ghost town—a town that once flourished but is now deserted

miners—workers who dig for diamonds or other natural resources

restored—rebuilt an object to look like it once did

restricted—made so only some people can access something

TO LEARN MORE

AT THE LIBRARY

Bodden, Valerie. *Ghost Towns*. Mankato, Minn.: Creative Education, 2018.

Owings, Lisa. *Battleship Island: The Deserted Island*. Minneapolis, Minn.: Bellwether Media, 2018.

Schuetz, Kari. *Bodie: The Gold-mining Ghost Town*. Minneapolis, Minn.: Bellwether Media, 2018.

ON THE WEB

FACTSURFER

Factsurfer.com gives you a safe, fun way to find more information.

1. Go to www.factsurfer.com.

2. Enter "Kolmanskop" into the search box and click 🔍.

3. Select your book cover to see a list of related web sites.

INDEX